THIS WALKER BOOK BELONGS TO:

_____

_____

_____

For Eilir
S.F-D.

First published 1992 by Walker Books Ltd
87 Vauxhall Walk, London SE11 5HJ

This edition published 2004

2 4 6 8 10 9 7 5 3 1

This book has been typeset in Berkeley

Printed in China

British Library Cataloguing in Publication Data:
a catalogue record for this book is available from the British Library

ISBN 1-84428-729-7

www.walkerbooks.co.uk

Moon frog

Animal Poems for Young Children

written by
Richard Edwards

illustrated by
Sarah Fox-Davies

WALKER BOOKS
AND SUBSIDIARIES
LONDON · BOSTON · SYDNEY · AUCKLAND

This Wasp

This wasp
and I
will not
be friends
until
its bad behaviour ends
and off
it buzzes
leaving me
in peace
to eat my jammy tea.

Seven Porcupines

Underneath the plum trees
Seven porcupines
Wait to catch the ripe plums
On their pointed spines.
When their spines are loaded
They run back to their den,
There to feed, there to feast,
There to slurp, and when
All the plums are safely
Stowed away in tummies,
And seven porcupines have said
Seven yummy yummies,
One by one they rattle out
Of their earthy den
To stand beneath the plum trees,
Catching plums again.

The Kangaroo

Every time
the kangaroo bounced
it muttered "Ouch!"
Serves it right
for keeping sharpened pencils
in its pouch.

The Heron and Rosanna

"Teach me how to cycle
And I'll teach you how to glide,"
Said the heron to Rosanna
By the sunny waterside.

Impossible, impossible,
But wait, look over there:
The heron on the saddle
And Rosanna in the air.

Keep Well Back

Keep well back,
Don't fall in,
Don't fall in
To the hippo's grin.

The hippo's grin
Is not so funny
When seen from in
The hippo's tummy.

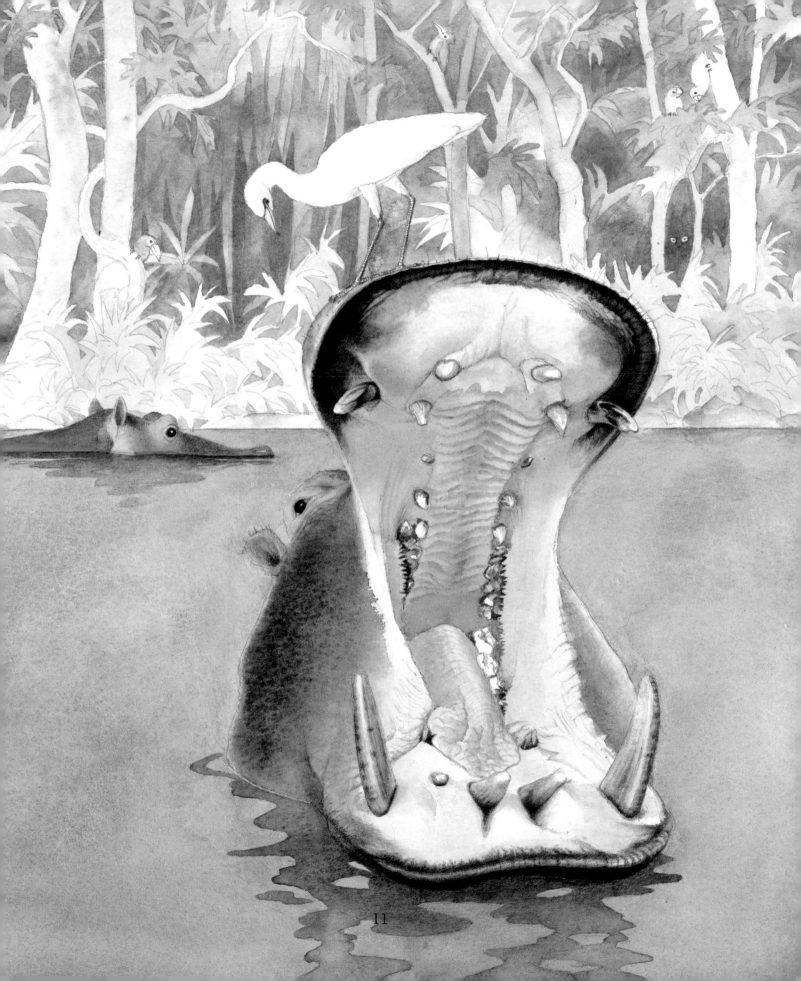

Banana Slug

Don't take a banana
If you picnic in the jungle
For it's in the deepest jungles
That banana slugs are found,
And if, while you are sheltering
Beneath a palm or banyan tree,
You put your peeled banana down
Beside you on the ground,
You might make a mistake when you
Pick up the peeled fruit to chew
And take a careless chomp
From a banana slug instead,
And if you do, it's true to say,
The taste will never go away
And even if you suck a mint,
Or chew Marmity bread,
Or lick a lolly, scrub your teeth,
Swill onion soup, or bite a peach,
Or try to rinse your sluggy mouth
With fruit juice from a jug,
Your gummy gums will never let
Your taste buds or your tongue forget
The savour, the full flavour
Of a fresh banana slug!

The Crocodile's Dentist

Here is his mirror, here is his drill,
Here is his briefcase, here is his bill,
Here are his boots on the riverbank, so
Where did the crocodile's dentist go?

Moon Frog

The moon slid down the sky,
The froggy whispered, "Soon,
If only it comes close enough,
I'll leap on to the moon."

The moon slid lower still,
The froggy paused, then – hop!
His long legs launched him at the moon
And landed him on top.

The moon sailed smoothly on
Along its starry course,
With froggy proudly riding
Like a jockey on a horse.

Midnight

In the moonlit music shop
Silk threads glisten,
Something's dropping slowly from the ceiling,
Listen!

Rattle tat
Tattle tat
Tattly tattly tattly
Rattle tattle
Tattle rattle
Rattly tattly rattly
Tattle tat
Rattle tat
Tattly tattly tum –

The spider
The spider
Dancing on a drum!

Ozzie Octopus

When Ozzie Octopus is sad –
An easy thing to be
When you are cold and lonely
At the bottom of the sea –
When Ozzie Octopus is glum
And far away from friends,
He stretches out his wavy legs
And curls them at the ends,
And soon starts laughing happily
And shaking just like jelly,
With all his eight legs tickling
His octopussy belly.

King of the Rock

I'm king of the rock,
Clear off or I'll knock
You down.

I don't like your face,
Clear off or I'll chase
You down.

My hooves are quick,
They click and kick.
My horns are long
And sharp and strong.
I'm brave. I'm bold.
My eyes are gold.

I'm chief. I'm the boss,
Clear off or I'll toss
You down.

The Café on the Corner

The café on our corner
Is different from most,
A lobster cuts the sandwiches,
A dragon browns the toast,
Retrievers fetch your order,
A walrus stirs your cup,
And elephants with soapy trunkfuls
Do the washing-up.

A Bee

A bee sleeps in my teapot,
But how does it get in?
It waits until I empty
All the tea-leaves in the bin.

A bee sleeps in my teapot,
But how does it get out?
It waits until the kettle boils
And buzzes down the spout.

Once I Saw

Once I saw a butterfly
Bigger than a plane,
It landed on a grassy hill
And then took off again,
And left behind its wing-prints
Pressed into the green
To prove that I had really seen
What I had really seen.

Once I saw a centipede
Bigger than a train,
It crawled into our garden
And then crawled out again,
And left one hundred footprints
To show where it had been
And prove that I had really seen
What I had really seen.

Cloud-sheep

I looked out of my window
And saw a cloud-sheep fly,
A woolly black-face cloud-sheep
Baa-baaing in the sky.

I looked out of my window
And heard the cloud-sheep say,
"I'm looking for my flock of friends,
Which way, which way, which way?"

I looked out of my window
And saw the cloud-sheep go,
Leaving wisps of wool behind
Like flakes of falling snow.

If I Were a Magician

If I were a magician,
I'd turn our local park
Into the plains of Africa
Where lions roar after dark,
And, standing on the bandstand roof,
I'd wave my magic wand
As herds of zebras queued to drink
Beside the boating pond.

Open All the Cages

Open all the cages,
Let the parrots fly –
Green and gold and purple parrots
Streaming up the sky.

Open all the cages,
Let the parrots out –
Screeching, squawking parrots swooping
Happily about.

Open all the cages,
Set the parrots free –
Flocks of parrots flapping homewards
South across the sea.

Silent trees in silent forests
Long for parrots, so –
Open all the cages,
Let the parrots go!

The White Bear

The white bear lopes
Over the slopes
Of snow.

The white bear's paws
Are tired,
They're going slow.

The white bear grunts,
Fifty more miles
To go.

The white bear lopes
Over the slopes
Of snow.

Where's the Fox?

Where's the fox?
Where's the fox?
Where is it hiding, where?
It's not in the wood or the
    wheatfield,
It's not in its stony lair.

Where's the fox?
Where's the fox?
Where has it gone to ground?
It's not in the ditch or the
    drainpipe,
The fox just can't be found.

Where's the fox?
Where's the fox?
How did we lose it, how?
It's run to the top of the rainbow,
And no one can catch it now.

30

Chameleons

Chameleons change colour to fit in with what's behind them;
A few are hiding quietly in this picture. Can you find them?

Tracks

Crows' feet, rabbits' feet, stoats' feet, rats' feet,
Foxes' feet, squirrels' feet, dogs' feet, cats' feet,
Long feet, short feet, bold feet, shy feet,
Wide feet, narrow feet, your feet, my feet,
Tracks in a circle, tracks in a row,
Tracks in a zig-zag, tracks in the snow.

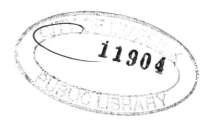

Mammoth

Once the snow stood on my back,
Once I was colossal,
Once my feet made glaciers crack,
Now I'm just a fossil.

Once I trumpeted and heard
Echoes ring the plain,
Once I felt returning spring
Changing snow to rain.

Once I waved my wild tusks high,
Once I was colossal,
Now I never see the sky,
Now I'm just a fossil.

Way Out West

"Imagine we're in Mexico,"
The snail said to the spider,
"And I'm your horse called Slidealong
And you're my cowboy rider.

There's trouble up in Greenhouse Gulch
And we've been asked to stop it
By rounding up some earwigs
And persuading them to hop it.

Put on your hat and sheriff's star,
Keep all your eight legs bandy
And saddle up, we're heading north
Across the Rio Grande."

The spider checked his boots and spurs,
Said "Yessir," and "Doggone it,"
Saddled the snail with a daisy leaf,
With one bound sprang up on it,

And off they rode at sundown
To bring back law and order
Beyond a row of cabbages
That marked the Texas border.

What Is a Skink?

What is a skink?
What do you think?
Can a skink swim
Or would a skink sink?
Does a skink gallop
Or does a skink slink?
What do skinks nibble?
What do skinks drink?

What is a skink?
What do you think?
Does a skink goggle
Or does a skink blink?
If the rain caught a skink
Would a skink shrink?
Is a skink purple
Or is a skink pink?
What *is* a skink?
What do you think?

The Worm Olympics

Once every four years on a night
That's warm and not too dark,
The worms hold their Olympics
In a corner of the park.

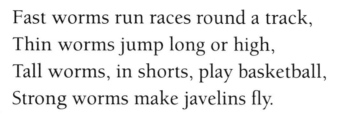

Fast worms run races round a track,
Thin worms jump long or high,
Tall worms, in shorts, play basketball,
Strong worms make javelins fly.

Some worms bowl bowls, some worms lift weights,
Some wrestle on a mat,
Some put the shot, some box and try
To knock each other flat.

Some line up by a dewy pool
To row or dive or swim,
Some worms are good at badminton,
Some worms are good at gym.

And all worms, when the games are over,
Proudly gather round
To cheer one last Olympic cheer
And vanish underground.

The Crab that Writes

When the tide is low on moonlit nights,
Out of the sea crawls the crab that writes,
Out of the sea crawls the crab whose claw
Writes these words on the shining shore:

PEBBLE MUSSEL
FIN AND SCALE
SOLE AND MACKEREL
SKATE AND WHALE
SEAWEED STARFISH
SALT AND STONE
SAND AND SHELL AND CUTTLEBONE.

When the tide is low on moonlit nights,
Back to the sea crawls the crab that writes,
Back to the sea crawls the crab whose claw
Leaves these words on the shining shore:

PEBBLE MUSSEL
FIN AND SCALE
SOLE AND MACKEREL
SKATE AND WHALE
SEAWEED STARFISH
SALT AND STONE
SAND AND SHELL AND CUTTLEBONE.

Pig

Pig, pig,
What have you brought me?

– Mud and a grunt and an oink.

Pig, pig,
What can I do
With mud and a grunt and an oink?

– With mud, said the pig,
You can wallow and play,
With a grunt, said the pig,
You can snooze all day,
With an oink, said the pig…
Then it dozed away.

So what can I do with this oink, I say,
What can I do with this oink?

Large and Little

The worker
ant
is light
and small,

The eleph-
ant
is big
and tall,

When eleph-
ant and worker
meet,
I hope
the eleph
minds its feet.

The Monkey King

I am the monkey king,
And I sit here all alone,
Trying to rule the monkey tribe
From my monkey throne.

I am the monkey king,
But the monkeys won't obey,
When I say: "Monkeys, gather round,"
The monkeys run away.

When I say: "Sit," they dance,
When I say: "Come," they go,
When I say: "Monkeys, shake my hand,"
They pull my little toe.

When I say: "Kneel," they jump,
When I say: "Sing," they wail,
When I say: "Monkeys, say your prayers,"
They tie knots in my tail.

Oh, I am the monkey king,
But I never asked to be,
If monkeys have to have a king,
Why me? Why me? Why me?

Index of first lines

A bee sleeps in my teapot 21

Chameleons change colour to fit in with what's behind them 30-31

Crows' feet, rabbits' feet, stoats' feet, rats' feet 32

Don't take a banana 12

Every time 8

Here is his mirror, here is his drill 13

I am the monkey king 42-43

If I were a magician 24

I looked out of my window 23

Imagine we're in Mexico 34-35

I'm king of the rock 18-19

In the moonlit music shop 16

Keep well back 10-11

Once every four years on a night 37

Once I saw a butterfly...22

Once the snow stood on my back.............................33

Open all the cages...25

Pig, pig..40

Teach me how to cycle...9

The café on our corner...20

The moon slid down the sky................................14-15

The white bear lopes...26-27

The worker...41

This wasp...6

Underneath the plum trees..7

What is a skink...36

When Ozzie Octopus is sad..17

When the tide is low on moonlit nights................38-39

Where's the fox...28-29

WALKER BOOKS is the world's leading
independent publisher of children's books.
Working with the best authors and illustrators
we create books for all ages, from babies
to teenagers – books your child will
grow up with and always remember. So…

FOR THE BEST CHILDREN'S BOOKS,
LOOK FOR THE BEAR